PLACE
MATCH

PLACE MATCH

The City Doctor's Guide to Finding Where You Belong

DR. KATHERINE LOFLIN

STORY FARM

Place Match: The City Doctor's Guide to Finding Where You Belong
© 2015 by Katherine Loflin
www.city-doctor.com
All rights reserved.

Published in the United States of America by Story Farm, LLC
www.story-farm.com

Library of Congress Cataloguing-in-Publication Data is available upon request.

ISBN 978-0-9966038-3-6

Printed in Canada

Designer: Lauren Eggert
Front cover design: Amanda Bardwell

Editor: Laura Baverman
Lead editor: Scott Morris
Copy editor: Laureen Crowley
Editorial assistant: Marcela Oliveira
Production management: Tina Dahl

10 9 8 7 6 5 4 3 2 1

First Edition, December 2015

For Grace

Without you, the best me would have not happened.
I love you.
Mommy and Gracie forever.

RELATIONSHIP
WITH PLACE

If you were asked to list the important relationships in your life, you would probably include spouse, partner, friends, co-workers and even pets. Your relationship to a place would most likely not be on the list—well, until now. When Katherine asked me to write a foreword to *Place Match: The City Doctor's Guide to Finding Where You Belong*, I agreed not only because she is my "placemaking BFF," a brilliant urbanist who shares my belief in the importance of great communities, but because I found the concept so compelling. Cultivating emotional, even romantic relationships, with place is an underexplored idea, and one that has the potential to speak to every human being.

I had never before thought of it, but it made perfect sense. I believe introducing this concept about "relationship with place" will initiate a refreshing new conversation about how we feel about a place and how we develop a relationship with a place. Why do we chose to live where we live and why do we want to stay—or leave?

Have you ever wondered why you live where you live? When you were young and living under your parents' roof or that of whoever raised you, you didn't have much of a choice where you lived. Yet you bonded with your place. The relationship you formed with your place likely became an important part of your identity: You were a city kid, a child of the suburbs, a country boy or girl. You adapted to your surroundings and started to form experiences, memories, rituals, habits about that place.

As adults, we don't always have a choice to live where we want due to economic, health, age or other reasons. In those cases, we just adapt to or adopt the place we live. But finding a relationship with place could bring happiness, stress-free living and a better quality of life.

If you could choose a place to live like you look for a mate, I suspect your decision-making process would be different. Developing a relationship with place could be one of the most fulfilling decisions you will ever make. Like any relationship, falling in love starts with a physical and emotional attraction followed by "getting to know you phase," or what some of us call dating. If the physical and emotional attraction is a match, the relationship is off to a great start.

For many generations—Greatest, Silent/Mature, Boomer and Gen X—it is not uncommon for some people either to remain in or nearby their place of birth. For others, moving away could be based on the place you went to college, to pursue a relationship or get a job. There are other factors in choosing a place too. Quality of schools, public safety and access to goods and services or weather, but establishing a relationship with a place—or how that place matches your personality—is not necessarily in the mix.

Something changed with Generation Y—the millennials. For the first time in American culture, a generation has placed a higher value on place. As crazy as it sounds, some millennials would find a place first before they have a job. Why would they do that? What are the millennials looking for? Experiences. They are looking for places that offer experiences that match their lifestyle preferences. If I had to generalize, older generations are consumers of goods, but younger generations (Generation X, Y and Z) are consumers of experiences. To form a relationship with place is about the experiences we expect in the neighborhood we choose to live in, the public spaces we plan to use, and the manner in which we travel from place to place. In any relationship, the day-to-day experiences affirm why we stay or confirm when it's time to move on.

Forming a relationship with place can be a key to contentment and an overall better quality of life. I can say firsthand that there are places where I have lived that have affected my emotional and mental state of mind and offered the full range of experiences. My hope is that understanding our relationship with place will change the way we choose a place to live. When you buy a house, you just don't buy a home, you buy the neighborhood, the town, the city and all the experiences it has to offer.

I am grateful Katherine has decided to share her insights and her personal story with the world. To see our connection to place in a new way is both exciting and refreshing. I am confident that after reading this book you will think differently about your relationship with place.

Mitchell Silver
NYC Parks Commissioner
Former President of the American Planning Association

CHAPTER 1

INTRODUCTION

People often ask me: "What's your favorite place?" It's a fair question given what I do. I work in the art and science of creating loved places—a field called placemaking. Still, I'm always reluctant to answer. My favorite place is personal and really shouldn't mean much to you, regardless of my expertise on what makes a good place.

Besides, my favorite place isn't one single place at all. My favorite place is the loved place—any place that is loved by the people who live there. Place is a hot topic these days. And lots of places are vying for your attention and presence. There's a whole consultancy niche now that helps cities create a place that may attract you, and I'm a part of it. But my position for cities has always been: Be who you are as a place, but be the best who you are you can be.

But I'm not writing this book for cities. I'm writing this book for you, resident. I want to help you find your loved place, your Place Match. In this era of livability, walkability, sustainable growth and placemaking, I want to help you know what to look for in order to call a place home.

Finding the right place to live is a lot like finding the right person with whom to share your life. I find that the marriage analogy is a good one, because now more than ever, your place is your partner. And like finding your marriage partner, where you live and put down roots is one of the most important decisions in your life.

For the past few years now there's been much more talk about good places to live, quality of life and the "live, work and play" nexus. There are polls, research and surveys in the media almost daily. And I've been on the front lines of this emerging field through my work on the Knight Soul of the Community project. As fate would have it, the John S. and James L. Knight Foundation funded what proved to be seminal research about the role of places in our lives during the nadir of one of the worst economic times in recent U.S. history: 2008-2010. Our two major research questions were: (1) what makes people love where they live, and (2) why does it matter?

But for now, know that as lead consultant and national expert for the project, one of my jobs was to help disseminate the findings throughout the country. As I did so, I was struck by how well the findings resonated with people. Of the many things I heard from residents as I traveled was a deep-seated disillusionment with work-life choices they had made so far in their lives, largely due to the recession. The refrain I often heard was, "I can make sacrifices for my job and in the end they don't really guarantee me anything. It can still end at any time and leave me high and dry." When jobs and homes were at risk or already gone, people became scared. And it caused some rethinking. Many of us seemed to be in the midst of a life shift.

> **"WHEN JOBS AND HOMES WERE AT RISK OR ALREADY GONE, PEOPLE BECAME SCARED.** AND IT CAUSED SOME RETHINKING. MANY OF US SEEMED TO BE IN THE MIDST OF A LIFE SHIFT."

I say "us" because that included me. I'll reveal more of my story throughout these pages, but the summary is that the community conversations I was having at work, especially during the last year of the project, mirrored my personal life at the time. My husband and I separated in mid-2010, just before the results of the final year of the Knight Soul of the Community project were publicized. Every time residents mentioned the disillusionment they felt, I connected with those feelings for a whole different reason. They felt the loss of security from their job investment and home investment—and so did I, from my marriage. Many of us were feeling left and lost.

And yet at the same time, I heard a new refrain during these conversations. It went something like this: "I will no longer live to work, but work to live." Residents wanted at least a balance in the work-life tug-of-war, and for many, life had finally won. With the clean start that unemployment—and in my case, divorce—provides, people were determined to rebuild their lives with a shifted set of values.

I remember early on in the Soul project, one of my first media requests came from a real estate publication. I hadn't considered the near universal appeal of the project so I was surprised to get such a request and said as much. The writer's response stuck with me and became one of my early key messages: "Today, houses are for sale everywhere. We now have to sell places."

During that time, many city branding and placemaking efforts began. Places were marketed like consumer products—with a brand image and a slogan designed to attract new residents and inspire loyalty among current ones.

Some of these efforts were confusing and felt gimmicky to residents. During a time when many residents were in flux and transitioning, such marketing helped them make the decision to stay or go. Meanwhile the Soul data revealed that upwards of 40 percent of residents felt no emotional connection to their place. In our community conversations there was a lot of talk of being "stuck in place," with an underwater home, a job that wasn't right or, increasingly, no job at all. What Soul provided these residents was validation of how they were feeling and the opportunity to identify, for the first time, what quality of life really meant to them.

During this time, I heard city leaders say to residents, "I know it's bad but we can make this work if you stay on and give it a chance," and residents would reply, "I can't risk any more on you." As I witnessed both, I was again reminded of the conversations that took place in marriages at critical junctures. And I realized how much we have underestimated the power of the relationship of person and place.

As time passed and Soul became a beacon project for understanding residents' relationships with their place and why it matters, the comparison between that relationship and a marriage or partnership only became stronger for me. Residents increasingly saw place as partner and were searching for or had found their Place Match. Add to that the ironic parallels between my professional life and personal life, and the idea for this book was born.

CHAPTER 2

THE SEARCH
FOR PLACE

There's this phenomenon that happens when I stand in front of a crowd of people and share the lessons I've learned over eight years studying cities and their residents.

I begin with the main findings of the Knight Soul project—that when people live in places that they find attractive, welcoming and full of opportunities for positive social interaction, they are likely in love with their place. I usually follow up with another reality about the role of place in our lives, one that surprises the older people in the room and affirms the young ones.

These days, I say, young talented people often choose place over a job.

At this point I usually see older folks shaking their heads in reaction, (although this happens less often as many have become aware of this new reality). It can't be true, those shaking heads seem to say. Or at least that it's hard to understand. Historically, people only moved to a place for a job, and it didn't matter where that place was or what it offered as a place.

"HISTORICALLY, PEOPLE ONLY MOVED TO A PLACE FOR A JOB, AND IT DIDN'T MATTER WHERE THAT PLACE WAS OR WHAT IT OFFERED AS A PLACE"

The young people have a different reaction. They nod their heads, and at least one stands up at the end of my talk and says, "That was me."

The millennial generation, and to some extent those in Generation X, started the important trend that has forever changed the conversation on place. Unlike previous generations, they choose places on purpose and carefully—they want vibrant night life, sprawling parks and plentiful recreation opportunities, music, entertainment and festivals, unique dining options and/or an active social scene. They want to live in a place where they feel welcomed and want to welcome others. Compelling career opportunities still matter, but many young people will sacrifice the best job offer for a better quality of life provided by a particular place.

A Gallup poll from 2010 shows that more than 50 percent of recent college graduates admitted to choosing places over jobs that year. And a study by Michigan Future Inc., a nonprofit and nonpartisan data source organization, ranked Illinois, California and New York as the top destinations for its college grads—53 percent of students said they chose the place they wanted to live over a job.

Psychology backs up our place needs

These statistics shouldn't really come as a surprise though. Turns out that we humans need to be in environments that suit us. Called ecological systems theory or person-in-environment fit, it's fundamental in the disciplines of social work and sociology, geriatrics and child development, anthropology and organizational psychology, public health and human psychology, and, increasingly, community design, architecture, land-use and smart growth planning.

This is the gist of both theories. We can't study humans without understanding the context of their environment, and we can't study environments without the context of the individual. We can't study humans without understanding the context of their environment, and we can't study environments without the context of the individual.

Developmental psychologist Urie Bronfenbrenner pioneered ecological systems theory. It suggests that besides the workplace, people are impacted by the entire microsystem around them—family, school, friends, a religious community, the neighborhood in which they live and to some extent, the political, governmental, religious and economic systems, the beliefs and values of those around them and the time period in which they live. Place plays a key role in most of those elements and affects the outcomes of the humans living in it.

For my city leadership clients, this is translated: Place matters and is integral to the overall success of the city and people living in it.

For the rest of us, it's about humans in an environment. It means that there are certain places where we feel at home and others where we simply don't, places where we feel we could thrive and places where we know we wouldn't. There are places where we feel belonging, and other places we don't. Though those environments may have similar qualities—beautiful surroundings, a great downtown, green spaces, diversity, good schools, manageable cost of living or reasonable taxes—different variations and manifestations of those qualities will appeal to different people, and in different ways. Think about it: that, too, is the person-in-environment fit.

Young people owned this before anyone else—and people like Richard Florida, the urban studies theorist who, though somewhat controversial today, started the conversation on place that we really needed to be having.

But the significance of place in our lives became all the more evident in 2008 and 2009, when the Great Recession destroyed the safety net of jobs and homes and bank accounts. What happened next was a convergence of the effect of the recession with the influence of the young talent changing the status quo on place. People who had turned their lives over to their jobs suddenly found that their jobs weren't there. The idea of building a life around work proved to be a serious mistake on many levels. Priorities were changing, and place quality—the environments where we live our lives—was quickly becoming more important than ever.

My best example—me

As has often been true on my journey with place, I was my best example. I left my home state of North Carolina straight out of the doctoral program at the University of North Carolina at Chapel Hill for a dream job in Miami at the Knight Foundation. Sure, I left North Carolina for a job, but I was leaving it for Miami—and how bad could that be? The word "Miami" immediately conjures visions of beautiful beaches, lively culture and endless adventures. Just getting that job at Knight in Miami made me feel like I'd made it. Plus, I was newly married. Life was good.

I was ready to fall in love with and marry Miami, as I had fallen in love with and married my husband. We were enamored and hopeful and ready for Miami. We wanted to have fun there and be attracted to all it had to offer. We wanted to feel accepted too. Although the parallel between relationship with partner and relationship with place hadn't dawned on me then, I now understand that we wanted from Miami what we had found in each other.

Later in life, my search for place took a different turn. Separated from my husband and with a 5-year-old daughter, I needed a different place partner. I had fallen out of love with where I was living, and my heart was broken. But more than just wanting to leave the place that now mostly symbolized heartache to me, I knew I wasn't getting what I needed from my place. And what I had always known to be true came into sharp focus: I wanted to raise my daughter, Grace, where I had been raised.

Just like we know when we've found the right place, we also know when we're in the wrong one.

The irony of it all was that just as marital divorce and place divorce were happening to me personally, professionally I was achieving success in the Knight Soul project. I spent my days

> **"I HAD FALLEN OUT OF LOVE WITH WHERE I WAS LIVING AND MY HEART WAS BROKEN.** BUT MORE THAN JUST WANTING TO LEAVE THE PLACE THAT NOW MOSTLY SYMBOLIZED HEARTACHE TO ME, I KNEW I WASN'T GETTING WHAT I NEEDED FROM MY PLACE."

talking about what makes people love where they live and why that's so important for our communities. I have to say I never felt more like a hypocrite—cheerleading love of place and no longer having that myself.

But the ironies were to become even more pronounced.

The fact that our relationship with place is like our relationship with a partner finally hit home, live on stage and, of all places, in Ottawa. I was doing a talk at the Federation of Canadian Municipalities in February 2012. And I was feeling especially determined that day—I was in the hometown of my estranged husband's new girlfriend and wanted to impress. As I stood before hundreds of city leaders from across Canada giving the presentation I wanted to give, the way I wanted to give it, something new slipped out. I went rogue and inserted an impromptu analogy that mirrored my own life at the time:

We have to try to figure out how we can be true to who we are as a place and let people be naturally attracted to that. But we also have to realize that as a place we will not be a perfect match for everybody. It's like any marriage. *(Pause as the irony hits.)* It's like any marriage. And we are discovering that the relationship a person has with place is in fact that kind of relationship."

Well, I amend that now to say that moment is exactly when I discovered "it": The fact is that finding your place is a lot like finding your partner. People search for places, they date them and maybe, eventually, they marry them. The marriage then requires commitment and work. And sometimes, the dynamics of the marriage change and the couple doesn't want to be married anymore. And eventually, that's OK.

Place Match, in today's world, is as critical as partner match. To say it was a "aha moment" is an understatement. Simultaneously, I noticed a dawning awareness in the crowd. People filed into the room from other sessions to hear my talk. It was standing room only. A transformation happened in the way I talked about place, and I knew it. And if I needed yet another sign, I got the tingly feeling from the back of my neck to the top of my head that has always been my personal telltale sign that I just hit a homerun. Something happened to me and something was happening in the room, and I knew my life would never be quite the same.

Yet, as I left the podium to rousing applause, a voice inside me heckled that I was a hypocrite. And so that day, I decided to finally practice what I preached—I began planning our move back to North Carolina. And by the time my plane touched down in Miami, I had 15 requests for speaking engagements in Canada and around the world.

CHAPTER 3

THE SEARCH
BEGINS

Any good relationship begins when two people who know who they are and what they want come together at the right place and time. It all starts with the soul searching required to figure out the first parts of that equation, and then the trial and error period, otherwise known as dating.

For young people, that typically happens between ages 18 and 24. It's the time in life when we're looking for a person and a place. And though that hasn't changed in decades, the way we search has changed dramatically. Today's young people search for a place by talking with their friends, watching videos and reading rankings and stories online. They care much less about the job they'll take—they're more apt to switch careers or workplaces within a year or two anyway. Finding the best place to live is just more important.

> **"TODAY'S YOUNG PEOPLE...CARE MUCH LESS ABOUT THE JOB THEY'LL TAKE—** THEY'RE MORE APT TO SWITCH CAREERS OR WORKPLACES WITHIN A YEAR OR TWO ANYWAY. FINDING THE BEST PLACE TO LIVE IS JUST MORE IMPORTANT."

These trends are reflected in the way millennials date too. Young people will date a person who lives across the country if it's the right match. They'll also date numerous people through online dating sites or mobile apps. Gone are the days where most marry the people they grew up with or met in college.

SEARCHING MEANS LETTING GO, AND SOMETIMES BOUNCING BACK

To find your Place Match, you have to date a place like you would a person in today's world.

And dating, over time, means being willing to latch on and move forward, or move on and let go.

That's true for both the people searching for places and the places themselves. Here's an example: On one of my visits, I had a heart-to-heart with a mayor who was bemoaning the loss of young people from his city. He wondered how to get them to stay. Like many people do when they're trying to impress a potential suitor, he tried to pretend his place had the attributes of a college town to mirror the places where his young people were moving. But he wasn't telling the truth about the opportunities in his city for people that particular age. He was trying to sell his place as something that it was not.

> **"ON ONE OF MY VISITS, I HAD A HEART-TO-HEART WITH A MAYOR WHO WAS BEMOANING THE LOSS OF YOUNG PEOPLE FROM HIS CITY.** ...I ENCOURAGED HIM TO STOP TRYING TO HOLD ON TO THEM WITH FALSE PROMISES—IF YOU ARE NOT A COLLEGE TOWN, DON'T PRETEND TO BE THAT."

I used a phrase we're so often told as young people on the search for a partner: "If you love something, let it go." But another saying is just as good: "Some things are just not meant to be."

I encouraged him to stop trying to hold on to them with false promises—if you are not a college town, don't pretend to be that. Recognize that those who leave may boomerang back to you, as many do. Stay connected to them while they're away dating other cities—make sure they know you'd still like to have them, and give them something authentic to come back to.

BE WHO YOU ARE, BUT BE THE BEST WHO YOU ARE

In the Knight Soul project, we called it "community attachment," an emotional connection to a place that transcends satisfaction to include loyalty and even passion and love for the place. That love is mostly driven by positive feelings about the social offerings, openness and aesthetics of a place. And when there are higher levels of community attachment, there are also higher levels of local economic growth, which powers the community to continue to provide that quality of life for residents.

You have to be strong in who you are to date and then marry, just like places must have a strong identity in order to attract and keep people who would be naturally attracted to what they have to offer. We tell our children throughout their lives: be who you are and don't let anyone change you or tell you you're not good enough. Now that doesn't mean that we don't expect our children and ourselves to continue to grow and develop. But it is a caution not to change the core of who you are for anyone. Instead, honor yourself and have confidence in who you are even as you change and grow.

And if someone is not a match for you, that's okay. Let him go. Let her go. Who knows? They may come back with a little more time and experience under their belts. My familiar refrain of "be who you are but be the best who you are that you can be" reflects this sentiment. And I find that places are often relieved to receive this advice.

It all hit home for me in several ways. I had a hard reality check after having my first child in 2007. I was on maternity leave from the Knight Foundation and though I loved my job, I dreaded leaving my daughter and returning to work. And so with the encouragement of my husband, who found me crying while looking at my business suits in the closet one day, I left my job at Knight and joined the ranks of the self-employed consultants. And as fate would have it, my first really big contract was with Knight and Gallup as the lead consultant on the Knight Soul of the Community project.

But another feeling started to plague me too—a deep yearning for my home state. We had always planned to move back to North Carolina when our daughter reached school age. And without my Knight job holding me in Florida anymore, the pull back to North Carolina became stronger. I knew Florida and I had given each other every opportunity, and though we were somewhat compatible, there was another place that was a better match for me, now more than ever.

Once we decide what we want during the search, we often struggle to be in a place or with a person that doesn't fit that desire. And some of us instead try to find the person or place that suits us. For me, the place was no longer Miami. It was back home in North Carolina.

HOW TO DATE YOUR PLACE

So what do you do when you're ready to date a place? First of all, remember that dating happens in steps and stages in order for a relationship to be built. It should happen over time so you can be sure your decision is the right one for you.

Here's what I suggest:

★ASK FRIENDS FOR RECOMMENDATIONS.

We do this all the time when we date. We ask our friends to set us up. We mine each other's friends on social media looking for people we're attracted to physically and who share our interests. We think, if so and so is a friend of this person, then he or she has to be all right. We trust the judgment of the people who know us when we're looking for a partner.

We should do the same when we're searching for a place.

The Soul project found that people recommend places they love—it's part of being attached to place. So when you ask friends about their city and they gush back about all the ways it'd be a fit for you, it's a pretty good sign. Or if friends are on social media sharing photos of their city and the activities they're participating in there or if they're always inviting you to visit their place, it's pretty clear they're loving it and want to show it off. This isn't just the case for young people—there's a trend of empty nesters moving into urban areas to take advantage of the social offerings and vibrancy. They're just as likely to brag on their place.

If your friends love a place, you might love it too.

★GET THE NEWSPAPER OR SUBSCRIBE TO A MEDIA SITE ONLINE.

Here you can dive deeper into those rankings you see in national media. While *Outside Magazine* might call a city tops for outdoor activities or *Parents* might name a place perfect for young families, local media lets you test those rankings. You can easily learn about the political and business climate, entertainment and dining options, the neighborhoods and schools and the overall culture of the place.

> **"JUST LIKE YOU SHOULD PROBABLY SEE YOUR POTENTIAL LIFE PARTNER WITH THE FLU BEFORE YOU MAKE A LONG-TERM COMMITMENT,** YOU HAVE TO LEARN ABOUT THE CHALLENGES OF THE PLACE, WHERE IT NEEDS CARE AND ATTENTION."

In the comments section, residents will speak up if they agree or disagree with the activities and assessments in local news.

There are also a growing number of monthly or quarterly local magazines about places. This trend seems to have started for the tourist audience, but a new crop of publications is designed for the resident. For example, the May 2015 issue of my hometown *Cary Magazine* had the cover story: "You Are Going to Love Living Here: A Guide for New Residents." Even if skewed to the Pollyanna, this gives the potential or new resident a place to start. Subscribing to those magazines online can also be helpful.

Media is a critical way for you, even from a distance, to start to date your place.

★RENT A HOME AND TRY IT OUT.

Dating your place doesn't mean you can't live there while you do. Young people do it all the time. They do some homework on the place from afar and show up and give it a whirl. That's not for everybody, though. But you can become a resident of a place and still be dating it.

We as a country are slowly letting go of the mentality that renters are bad. In the Soul project, we found that renters in some cities had higher attachment to their place than the homeowners. Fact is that the housing collapse, weak economy and life needs have made renting the most viable option for many people, regardless of income, age, stability and even their intentions with the place. I rented a house for years when I came back to North Carolina. I still had high attachment to the area, and I'm generally a respectable person.

★DISCOVER WHAT IT HAS TO OFFER AND HOW THAT MAKES YOU FEEL.

We've all been on good dates and bad dates, ones where we feel an inexplicably strong connection and ones where we feel nothing. This is not the difference between a good or bad person. It has to do with how we feel in the presence of the person.

Similarly, for you to know if you can make a long-term commitment to a place you have to get there and learn what it has to offer. And a place has to put itself out there for you to know that. So how easy is it to get to know that place? What are your discoveries? Just like with first dates, smart cities usually try to show off their strengths, especially to visitors or tourists. But you have to work past that when you are dating a city.

Just like you should probably see your potential life partner with the flu before you make a long-term commitment, you have to learn about the challenges of the place, where it needs care and attention. Do you still feel that connection to the place despite its shortcomings? Do you feel yourself wanting to be the "chicken soup" for the place? Do you love it enough to want to help?

Finally, how easy is it for you to get to know that place and feel accepted or welcomed? There are some places where residents still apologize for being a "new resident," having only lived there 20+ YEARS (!). It's said half-jokingly, but there is also some hard truth behind those feelings.Some places aren't very helpful when it comes to getting to know about them or fitting into them. If you can't get to know the place, if you feel a sense of disconnection or you feel unwelcome, that's something to take seriously.

Now when I talk about a place being welcoming, this does not mean it has to be gushy. Think about it. Some people are touchy-feely, they ask a lot of questions or they talk a little too close for comfort. The same can be true for cities. In North Carolina, you may be stopped in the grocery store aisle by a stranger asking where you got your shirt, handing you the keys you dropped or offering a suggestion for how to cook the perfect corn on the cob. Some people love that. Some, not so much. Some feel like they are a welcomed part of the city's fabric and culture without feeling the need to discuss it.

When I first moved to Miami, I was in the grocery store

with a colleague who looked on in horror as I said hello to people I passed in the aisle, something that is commonplace in my hometown. She asked if I knew these people, and I responded "No." She then informed me that people don't say hi to those they don't know, but once they've met you, you're forever greeted with kisses.

When I'd visit my family in North Carolina and run to the store for something, someone would say hello to me and I had to remember to get back in "NC mode," as I would call it. I wouldn't be kissed as much as in Miami, but I did need to remember to say hello.

HOW NOT TO DATE YOUR PLACE

★ **DON'T DECIDE TO MOVE TO A PLACE BASED ON VACATION EXPERIENCE(S) THERE.**

Living in a place can be much different than visiting a place. Have you ever heard someone say: "It's a great place to visit, but I wouldn't want to live there"? That is a real thing.

"NOW WHEN I TALK ABOUT A PLACE BEING WELCOMING, THIS DOES NOT MEAN IT HAS TO BE GUSHY. THINK ABOUT IT. SOME PEOPLE ARE TOUCHY-FEELY, THEY ASK A LOT OF QUESTIONS OR THEY TALK A LITTLE TOO CLOSE FOR COMFORT. THE SAME CAN BE TRUE FOR CITIES."

Vacation is a great way to get a feel for a place, and you should visit a place before you decide to live there. But that cannot be the extent of the dating you do with that place.

It would be like meeting someone on a first date and then immediately eloping to Las Vegas. The truth is that many places with tourist-based economies offer a better life for visitors than for the residents. That makes visitors jump to the conclusion that it is the place for them. You have to dig deeper to get know the place. Be sure to talk to residents of the place about what it's like to live there, not just to the people who love visiting there.

★DON'T TRUST TOP 10 LISTS.

Today a city is No. 1 on a list. Tomorrow that same city didn't break the top 100 on another. There are two lists published this week on walkability, and a city is listed as No. 2 on one and No. 32 on another that is supposedly based on the same metric. So what's up with these lists?

The proliferation of "city lists" only reaffirms the increasing power of place in our lives. But they can be confusing, subjective and sometimes downright silly. You shouldn't base too much of your decision-making on them. And I say that as a resident of a place that usually ranks high on most of them.

Creators of these lists each use their own definitions and metrics (usually based on the data readily available or provided by a sponsor). So walkability can be based on a "walk score" or the availability and quality of sidewalks. Family-friendly could be based on the policies of local employers or teacher quality and retention. You have to read the fine print or else take each list with a grain of salt.

But perhaps most importantly, those lists don't tell you much about whether a city is your Place Match. There is the "on paper" place and then the "on the ground" place. For example, if you are seeking a family-friendly city and you see a list of the Top 10 Family Friendly Cities in the U.S., does that mean the No. 1 place on that list is where YOUR family would be the happiest? Maybe, or maybe not. You have to get "boots on the ground," and not just on vacation.

Similarly, lots of places have great social offerings, openness and aesthetics. But it is how they are translated in the place that you need to connect to and love. Miami's social life looks much different than Raleigh's. It can even look different in neighboring cities! That's why a list or a visit can't be enough in finding your Place Match. Each yields valuable information on the place, but none of them alone can be decision-makers.

The journey to find your Place Match starts out with a search for place candidates, based on research both online and on the ground, with the help of friends as well as personal experience. As you explore, you will learn important things about your place candidates, which will result in you either wanting to learn more or having learned enough to take them off your list.

As we all know, dating can be challenging but also exciting. And just like dating people, dating places as a visitor and even as a new resident is an important and necessary process to grow love for the place, and eventually, to consider making a commitment.

CHAPTER 4

FINDING THE
PLACE MATCH

You might have picked a place and you're living there, but you haven't made a long-term commitment yet. In many ways, you're still dating your place. Maybe you're still trying to make friends and meet your neighbors. Maybe you're exploring and seeing where you feel connection. You're learning the best way to get where you want to go. You may be getting lost, a lot.

If you're outdoorsy, you might be trying out trails or interest groups to find a good match. You're using your work connections or new acquaintances to search for a new doctor, hairstylist, grocery store and mechanic. If you're spiritual, you're probably looking for a religious community. If you have kids in school, you're learning how the school works and which parents are most likely to be your friends. You're wandering the downtown or seeing what's walkable from your home. You're learning a great deal along the way.

Some of these experiences will be hits, but some will be misses. And those experiences send messages to your brain about your match with the place. As they should—it takes time to learn and integrate into a new place, even after you've searched and dated.

Sound familiar? Once we feel comfortable enough to call someone a boyfriend or girlfriend, that doesn't mean we're ready to call that person a husband or wife. New relationships, even serious ones, still require dating, just like new places require dating. And really, it's a continuous, never-ending process, even after you've determined you've met "The One."

So what makes you fall in love with your place? How do you know it's your Place Match?

It's going to be different for each of us, but it all comes down to your compatibility with the narrative (or soul) of the place. Then, how does that grow over time? It's best when places make it easy to see who they are.

Here's what I mean:

Fort Wayne, Indiana. During the Knight Soul project, I was often asked for the best examples of what places did with the findings. Top of that list was always Fort Wayne.

"THE CITY STARTED SMALL. BUT STARTING SMALL IS USUALLY THE SMARTEST WAY TO GO. WHEN PEOPLE CAN SEE PROGRESS, THEY WANT TO DO MORE AND ATTRACT OTHERS TO GET INVOLVED."

Fort Wayne is in north-eastern Indiana, at least two hours from Indianapolis, Detroit and Chicago, with a population of about 260,000. Fort Wayne realized that leveraging place is key to its future. And all sorts of leaders in the community rallied around that idea. All types of residents, from artists and young entrepreneurs, to seasoned business people and politicians, joined together to allow love of place to guide efforts to make a difference for the whole.

Here are some examples. The first involves fresh-baked cookies. For nearly 15 years, residents (usually retired) called Hospitality Hosts are posted the arrival gates at Fort Wayne International Airport. They hand out locally made cookies to visitors and welcome them to Fort Wayne. Whether you're tired, struggling with a bag, hot or cold, distracted, hungry, irritated, late or longing to be home, imagine someone welcoming you and handing you a cookie. You have to smile and think: "Wow, how about that."

I've been the recipient of these treats many times, and it always sets the tone for my visit. Just like I used to have to be reminded to get back into "NC mode" on my visits home, this small act always reminds me that I'm in Fort Wayne. And it's left an impression on me ever since. It is a more authentic representation than the expected "welcome" sign at most airports.

When I first visited Fort Wayne with the Knight Soul project, residents had a growing passion and focus on place. Soul had provided the framework of understanding and a road map to go forward. As Mayor Henry said to me on that visit: "Our instincts were telling us we were doing the right thing [by being more place-focused], but data helps us to move forward with confidence and evidence."

Of course, sometimes there were unintended consequences, like when the city invited people to suggest names for the new government center in 2010. A large percentage of the population participated, with nearly 24,000 votes in favor of naming the building after a former longtime mayor of the city. Sounds great, right? There was a problem though—that mayor's name was Harry Baals (pronounced "Balls"). And the closest runner up suggestion hadn't even garnered 600 votes.

Not surprisingly, Fort Wayne leadership was a bit reticent to name their nice new acquisition the Harry Baals Government Center. When the leaders decided against the popular vote, the good-natured backlash from the public began—the name won fair and square after all. And the prominent ringleader of this position was Jimmy Kimmel. He did a personal plea on his late show for the name suggestion to be honored. The Mayor even appeared on his show in 2011 to defend his choice not to honor the people's vote.

As a result, the city of Fort Wayne enjoyed some national and international exposure. Today, you can visit the building called Citizens Square, the name that received five votes. But the story lives on via a popular T-shirt the city designed that said, "You already know Fort Wayne has Baals. Come see our other assets." I still wear mine.

These anecdotes are great examples of what to look for in a city. In many cases, it's the small yet meaningful things. In 2013—after the Harry Baals incident—when leaders had commissioned sculptural bicycle racks in celebration of the 50th anniversary of its local university, Indiana University-Purdue University Fort Wayne. The city installed 50 locally created racks downtown to encourage exploration and promote cycling. Today, you can get a map of the bike rack locations and use it as a guide to discover downtown destinations.

And Fort Wayne isn't stopping there. There is a growing young professional and youth engagement culture through Fort Wayne's Young Leaders of Northwest Indiana. New development downtown and on the riverfront is underway. All sectors are finding their role and contributing to create a place-focused city. The city started small. But starting small is usually the smartest way to go. When people can see progress, they want to do more and attract others to get involved.

PLACE MATCH MEANS ECONOMIC VITALITY

It didn't take long for Fort Wayne to start to see results. The population has grown each year since 2010. There's a low unemployment rate. The city has also been named on various lists—11th best "Opportunity City" to make your mark by *Forbes*, top 10 best quality of life by Nerdwallet, fifth best children's zoo by *Parents* magazine and top 10 up and coming cities for college grads according to Zip Recruiter. You probably remember that I usually advise against judging a city by lists like these, but in the case of Fort Wayne, these accolades seem to ring true.

> **"THAT KIND OF COMMITMENT TO PLACE YOU CAN'T BUY, CAJOLE, MANUFACTURE, BARTER OR STEAL.** IT COMES FROM AN AUTHENTIC LOVE OF PLACE AMONG FOLKS WHO HAVE FOUND THEIR PLACE MATCH."

New businesses have opened in town, and young talent is staying after high school and college. They have been inspired by the energy in the town. I have witnessed young entrepreneurs say publicly (some in khakis, some in tattoos, some in-between) that no place would have allowed them to succeed in starting their own business like Fort Wayne has— they will stay and give back because of it. I have seen young talent acknowledge the city's challenges and yet promise to stay and be a part of the solutions. That kind of commitment to place you can't buy, cajole, manufacture, barter or steal. It comes from an authentic love of place among folks who have found their Place Match.

They feel optimistic about Fort Wayne because they are investing in its future.

So as you continue to date your place, how do you know you are ready to make a long-term commitment? If some days are great and some days aren't, then how will you know you've found your Place Match? Just like in a serious relationship, do you break up after a bad day? Probably not. But if there is more unhappiness than happiness, you will start to consider if maybe you two don't belong together after all.

So what makes you know a place is where you belong?

We'll look deeper at that question in the next chapter.

CHAPTER 5

HOW TO KNOW IT'S THE ONE

et's look a bit deeper into the ways we get attached to a place. Findings from the Knight Soul project made clear that some of the most important things that make us love where we live are the aesthetics, welcomeness and the social offerings of a place. Now it is time to consider if you've loved those things as you've dated your place.

DO YOU FIND YOUR PLACE BEAUTIFUL?

If you're in your Place Match, you should love the aesthetics of the place—the charm, natural beauty, architecture, parks, trails, downtown, skyline (or even lack of one). In an aesthetically pleasing city, leaders also recognize the importance of green spaces and smart development even during budget crunches. There's an understanding that decay and blight undermines that. Where does your leadership stand?

We derive a lot from the environment we live in. It is the basis of our relationship with our place and can set a tone for everything that happens within it. The Soul research findings really helped to highlight the reality that environment matters in growing love of place. It's not "extra" but integral.

DO YOU THINK THE PLACE IS OPEN AND WELCOMING?

Having a sense of belonging in a place is a powerful force in attaching us. And it's not that we are tolerated, which means "I put up with you." True openness means, "You are welcome." And I don't just mean welcoming to different types of people. I am also talking about people in different stages of life— seniors, young talent, singles and families with young children. One way we convey welcomeness is in place design. For example, how easy to navigate are sidewalks for a family with a stroller, a kid trying to get to campus, a senior to a grocery store or a person who walks to work? It's also about the availability of goods, services and businesses for different types of people in different phases of life.

Of course, when it comes to making a newcomer feel welcome, nothing can replace the attitudes of the residents. That's right, dear resident, you are not off the hook. How we treat each other on the roads, in the grocery store and at Little League games contributes to the openness of the place. For some folks, Place Match will involve lots of honking, hustle-bustle and less interaction with strangers. But for others, the opposite will be true.

Businesses are starting to use these aspects of places to decide where they will open an office and hire workers. They want to see how well they could sell the place to the desired pool (if they don't already live there). One way to measure a city is to test out the welcomeness of the place in these experiential ways. Have you done this? How well did the place sell you?

"NO PLACE IS PERFECT. BUT THE THINGS THAT A PLACE DOES PARTICULARLY WELL SHOULD MATCH WHAT YOU MOST WANT IN THAT PLACE. ...INTERESTINGLY, THESE THINGS OFTEN PARALLEL WHAT WE'RE LOOKING FOR IN THE PEOPLE WE DATE OR MARRY."

FINALLY, DO THE SOCIAL OFFERINGS APPEAL TO YOU?

Humans are social beings, albeit in different ways sometimes. Perhaps then it's not surprising that the

Soul project found that having social offerings that appeal to you is most important to growing your love of place. The basic questions here are: Can you do what you want to do in this place? And can you do it in the way you want? Because it's not just about social infrastructure like the night life, food scene and shopping options, it's also about your experience there. If it's hard to get around and park your car, if you're treated poorly or feel unsafe or uncomfortable or just feel worse for having done something, you will likely not want to do it again, even if it's an activity you enjoy.

Every place has social offerings. As you've dated your place and participated socially, have you enjoyed the experience?

COMPATIBILITY IS KEY

No place is perfect. But the things that a place does particularly well should match what you most want in that place.

Interestingly, these things often parallel what we're looking for in the people we date or marry.

Think about it. Your ideal partner should be someone you find attractive, who you feel accepts you and is fun to do things with. If you feel your partner is always trying to "change you" (physically or otherwise), then you will feel rejection more than belonging. If you prefer a quiet dinner and a movie at home and your partner wants to hit the club at 11 p.m., then you will likely not enjoy each other's social choices. The goal is to find compatibility in these areas. Then love for each other will grow naturally. The same is true with your relationship with place.

So how should you feel about your place? What does love of place feel like?

We found in the Knight Soul project that this manifests in a few different kinds of specific feelings or behaviors:

- You brag about or recommend the place to others.

- You feel optimistic about the place's future.

- You feel that it's the perfect place for you.

- You have a sense of pride in the place and look forward to showing it off to your friends and family.

- You feel satisfied living there.

Your Place Match should grow those feelings in you over time.

So how long should it take to know if a place is the one?

For some, it might happen quickly. But our research for the Knight Soul project showed an attachment bump for many residents around the three- to five-year mark. And if you think about it, that's about the same lifespan as any serious personal relationship—dating (or even job!). Around that time, you're deciding if you're ready to make a long-term commitment to a person or if it's best to move on. A lot of marriages hit a crossroads around that time too.

COMPATIBILITY ISN'T PERFECTION

I have certainly felt hypocritical at times that I didn't walk my own talk of placemaking.

I have lived in places I didn't love.

I have even felt disconnected at times from places I did love.

My daughter and I have jumped in the car for school out of convenience and only walked there during the annual "Walk to School" Day. And often, I've felt an internal nagging as a result.

It just goes to show that all of us—even those of us who focus on place for a living—can be an example of what's right or wrong about our relationship with place. Same as a relationship with a partner: Some days we get it right, and some days we don't. Some days we feel in sync, some days we want to isolate. Some days we feel that person is our perfect match, some days we question our choice. Some days we feel the love, some days we fight.

That's okay. It's what makes our relationship with place like any other important relationship in our life. And it is why this decision deserves so much thought and consideration before we make a commitment.

> **"SOME DAYS WE FEEL THE LOVE, SOME DAYS WE FIGHT. THAT'S OKAY. IT'S WHAT MAKES OUR RELATIONSHIP WITH PLACE** LIKE ANY OTHER IMPORTANT RELATIONSHIP IN OUR LIFE. AND IT IS WHY THIS DECISION DESERVES SO MUCH THOUGHT AND CONSIDERATION BEFORE WE MAKE A COMMITMENT."

CHAPTER 6

THE SYMBIOTIC
RELATIONSHIP

A young Raleigh man named Matt Tomasulo, passionate about his city's revival of restaurants, museums, apartments and shopping, did something bold a couple years ago.

As city leaders sat in City Hall conference rooms discussing the lack of walkers on the streets despite all the new offerings, Tomasulo took action, hanging 27 easy-to-understand way-finding signs on utility poles at three major intersections. He wanted to show downtown visitors how long it would take to walk to nearby destinations.

And within days his project became the talk of Facebook. It got mentions in national and global media outlets, and cities around the world reached out to copy the project.

And here's the kicker. Tomasulo never asked for permission.

Now, that proved fateful in some ways. Somebody complained to the city, asking if Tomasulo had a permit for the signs. The city eventually ruled the signs illegal and removed them. But Walk Raleigh had rallied enough of a crowd to get 1,300 signatures on a petition to bring them back. Mitchell Silver, then Raleigh's City Planner and now the New York City Parks Commissioner (who also wrote the foreword of this book!), realized the signs were a great idea. So he and the city responded by changing the law and reinstalling them. Now, Walk [Your City] has seed funding from the Knight Foundation to expand into new cities. And in late summer of 2015, Tomasulo announced he was running for Raleigh City Council.

I love this story. I love it because Tomasulo understood that placemaking isn't just about the initiatives by the city or its elected officials. Tomasulo saw something he could do to change perceptions about the place, and also help it be more welcoming and more social, and he just did it. I love it because leaders like Silver get that part of their jobs are to find a way to "get to yes" when residents step up, engage and show innovative initiative for community benefit. Lastly, I love it because it shows that great placemaking ideas don't have to be costly or complicated to have impact.

To me, this story shows another critical part of Place Match. Once you find your Place Match, you are in partnership with that place. Leadership has a responsibility to make the place great, and so do you. You are in it together.

> **"IT'S A SYMBIOTIC RELATIONSHIP. YOU CONTRIBUTE TO IT, IT CAN CONTRIBUTE BACK TO YOU, THE ATTACHMENT GROWS** AND BOTH BENEFIT. JUST LIKE IN A HEALTHY MARRIAGE: YOU DO FOR ME, I DO FOR YOU, AND TOGETHER WE CONTRIBUTE TO CREATING A BETTER WHOLE, WHICH SOLIDIFIES OUR BOND."

Again, the comparison to marriage almost writes itself. In order for a marriage to work, both parties have responsibilities and expectations to keep the partnership healthy. How that shakes out is different for each marriage. Historically, it fell along traditional gender lines—the man works the long hours, takes out the trash and mows the lawn, while the woman cooks, cleans and raises children.

In many modern marriages, the responsibilities are more blended. One spouse might take on more chores when the other has a tough week at work. One might drive around the kids while the other preps and cleans up after meals. The key is that both parties agree on the arrangement and execute their responsibilities for the betterment of the relationship and to keep the match intact.

The same goes for cities and their residents. The relationship will be different in each place. It will also ebb and flow— sometimes the city takes leadership in building place, other times the residents generate and execute ideas that optimize the place.

WHAT CITIES CONTRIBUTE TO PLACE

But let's start with the role the city might play in the Place Match. First, and importantly, the city creates the budget— the set of financial priorities for the city in a given year.

Now traditionally, a city may prioritize public safety, infrastructure, transportation or education, especially in a budget crunch. But a key determination of the Knight Soul project was the importance of aesthetics and social offerings in attaching residents to their place. Historically, these are the perceived "softer" features of place that are first to be cut when budgets get tight.

Knight Soul findings helped city leaders realize that things like aesthetics and social offerings matter to developing our love of place. And residents' love of place seems to be related to the economic vitality of a city. As attached residents choose to spend more time in their place (instead of traveling elsewhere) and invite others to join them there, more people spend time and money in the place. Attached residents were also found to be more satisfied in their jobs—that helps with talent retention and productivity.

All of these contribute to the bottom line of the place, which affords more opportunities to make the place lovable to its residents and visitors. It's a symbiotic relationship. You contribute to it, it can contribute back to you, the attachment grows and both benefit. Just like in a healthy marriage: You do for me, I do for you, and together we contribute to creating a better whole, which solidifies our bond.

WHAT RESIDENTS CONTRIBUTE TO PLACE

Another role cities can play is to promote the efforts of residents or organizations that contribute to placemaking. Here's a good example:

In the small rural town of Macon, Georgia, an effort to make the city more inclusive led to Macon Money. The brainchild of a gaming company (and funded by Knight), this real-world game involved bonds worth an unknown dollar amount between $10 and $100, split in half and distributed to residents. In order to "cash" the bonds at local businesses, residents had to find the holder of the other half of their bond through a website, social media or by chance in person. They were encouraged to spend the cash together once a match was made. The currency itself was designed to reinforce community bond and identity—it portrayed symbols of the community's narrative.

Macon Money won an international award for innovation and enjoyed international press because of it. And a report was completed afterward to analyze its impact.

A key finding of that study was that Macon Money contributed directly to place attachment, as participants said it made them more optimistic about the future of Macon. Businesses benefited from that too. Nearly half the participants visited places they'd never been before, and most went back again after the fact.

And that brings us to the resident's role in making the Place Match. One key way is by embracing efforts that showcase the place, ones that lift up and honor the story of that place.

As cities recognize the impact of place-centered approaches on vitality and economic growth, the stories are growing in number. And they are certainly not limited to this country.

In Newfoundland, residents created a program called [HERE]SAY to relay the place narrative through oral histories and storytelling and to encourage residents to be welcoming and to bond to their place. All around St. John's and Torbay there are signs that encourage passersby to "hear about here"—the signs provide a local phone number to call to hear a recorded story of what happened in that particular spot in history, told from the mouths of its residents. The goal was to build a collection of "Story Maps" that make the place come alive, rather than

> **"IT'S IMPORTANT FOR YOU TO ENGAGE IN YOUR PLACE MATCH IN A WAY THAT'S MEANINGFUL** AND DOABLE FOR YOU. EVERY CONTRIBUTION MATTERS. WHETHER IT'S BY HOLDING A DOOR FOR SOMEONE...OR CREATING AN APPRECIATION OF YOUR PLACE IN YOUR KIDS, WHATEVER WORKS FOR YOU, COMMIT TO DOING IT."

just offering the geographic location of streets or buildings or landscape. It won a national award for excellence in public presentation of historic places.

In Grand Rapids, a young man named Rob Bliss created a series of events to put his city in a positive light after it was misrepresented in national press. His projects include a lip dub video (viewed over 5.5 million times on YouTube) and a statewide singalong. He's also credited with starting the giant waterslide trend in 2010. He installed a 500-foot slide on a downtown street—it was believed to be "the world's longest waterslide" at the time. It was free to any resident, and thousands showed up. The event grabbed international attention and made those who participated proud of their city's ingenuity. A Salt Lake City startup company has since launched an event series now hitting cities around the nation with 1,000-foot street-long waterslides.

"CLEARLY, RESIDENTS PLAY A TREMENDOUS ROLE IN CREATING THE ENERGY OF A PLACE. IT'S DONE BY HOW WE TREAT EACH OTHER, OUR CIVILITY AND HOW WE WELCOME OTHERS TO THE PLACE. IT'S BY TAKING PRIDE IN THE PLACE, AND IT'S BY ENGAGING WITH THE PLACE IN A WAY THAT HAS A POSITIVE IMPACT, EITHER BIG OR SMALL."

Clearly, residents play a tremendous role in creating the energy of a place. It's done by how we treat each other, our civility and how we welcome others to the place. It's by taking pride in the place, and it's by engaging with the place in a way that has a positive impact, either big or small.

It's important for you to engage in your Place Match in a way that's meaningful and doable for you. Every contribution matters. Whether it's by holding a door for someone, helping a mom carry her stroller down the subway stairs or creating an appreciation of your place in your kids, whatever works for you, commit to doing it.

In previous chapters, I've shared that I have not always felt that connection to place, that I've felt guilty for not always walking my own talk about place. But the last few years of my life have been committed to changing that, starting with my move back to North Carolina. My new home is located on what is one of the last remaining two-acre intact lots in my area—one acre developed, one not. It makes me feel like I'm helping to honor the green spaces, and I'm happily joined by neighbors who are doing the same.

Additionally, my daughter, Grace, now commutes to school on foot. It's nice to be able to walk the talk (literally) about the importance of connection to place in this tangible way. She loves it and thinks she's approaching rock star status as her friends pass in cars and yell "hi" out the window and parents cheer their approval as well. She's supported and I know watched over as she walks the small trek each way daily.

I especially enjoy showing my North Carolina to my daughter—sharing things that I did as a kid, taking her to mountain destinations I frequented, telling her stories about the place. It is thrilling to walk her in the steps I took growing up here, and it is rewarding watching her forge her own path of appreciation and love for this place.

I also brought Jane's Walk to Raleigh. Jane's Walk is a great way to encourage discovery of your place alongside your fellow residents. In honor of the birthday of place pioneer Jane Jacobs, walks are designed and led by residents to get "boots on the ground" in their place the first weekend in May. Though I brought the international program to Raleigh as a gift to my place, the effect on both me and other organizers has been nothing short of transformational. But more on that later. My point is these have been contributions to place that worked for me. Yours may be similar, or different. But they all matter.

When you contribute to the quality of your place, you come to love it even more and the place rewards your efforts with providing you an environment in which you thrive. A special partnership to be sure.

CHAPTER 7

THE RELATIONSHIP
OVER TIME

It doesn't matter what age we get married or start dating—our relationships change over time. And it's because people change over time. By choice, we change our jobs, friends and interests. Other things change with the simple progression of time—like health or personality or even the way we communicate and express ourselves. Things happen as we experience life. And any of these changes or all of them combined can make or break a relationship.

I wrote earlier that a Place Match could take three to five years to establish. That same life cycle seems to happen once you've found a match too. Even after Soul concluded, I continued to talk to people about their relationship with place. And I've learned a lot from folks at different stages with their place, including those that felt love of place waning over time. Again and again those people told me a key reason for the shift is a

"YOU WILL HAVE BAD DAYS IN A PLACE, EVEN IN YOUR PLACE MATCH. BUT ONE BAD WEEK IN A PLACE DOESN'T MEAN IT'S OVER, JUST LIKE ONE FIGHT DOESN'T EQUAL DIVORCE. IF THE MATCH IS SUSTAINABLE—LIKE A MARRIAGE—IT'LL BOUNCE BACK."

realization that the place has changed, that "this place just isn't what it used to be". They feel a palpable loss as a result. Some people choose to stay anyway—they either don't have the economic means to leave or it's all they have known for so long. Others have the opportunity to leave, and do.

It all calls to mind a refrain often heard at the end of a marriage: "This is not the person I married."

For me, both marriage and love of place unraveled near the same time. The latter happened after my daughter was born, and a self-fulfilling prophecy began to play out in my mind. My husband and I had always said we'd move back to North Carolina when our daughter hit school age. But pretty suddenly—and perhaps largely due to my research for the Knight Foundation—I began to notice all the ways in which Miami wasn't the match for my family. I had changed, my life had changed and it was time to go.

For my aesthetics, I needed fewer high-rise buildings and more of a neighborhood feel. For my social offerings, I wanted farmer's markets and family movie nights and fewer nights out that started at 10 p.m. And though I always appreciated the big city feel of Miami, I now longed for civility and the way of life I had known growing up in North Carolina.

My marriage also didn't stand the test of time—things had happened, mistakes had been made on both sides and a commuting marriage was forced on us when we couldn't sell our Miami house, which created a hard blow. Our union was stressed, and then it was broken.

WHAT TO DO WHEN RELATIONSHIPS CHANGE

So what are our options when our relationship with our place changes? Well, they aren't much different than when any marriage changes.

First, I think it's only fair to do real soul searching before making any drastic decisions. To my clients, I often suggest the "Is it true?" strategy for deciding the first step in place intervention. Residents are usually not shy about voicing their opinions about aspects of any place, good or bad. However, a key question remains: are these opinions true about the place? They can ask, for example, "Is it true that a park is unsafe at night or that some people don't feel welcome there?" and if the answer is yes, the place has some work to do. But even if they ask that question and the perception is not true, place leaders must work to change that perception. After all, people act off their perceptions, reality or not.

As residents, perceptions and reality impact our love of place. Perhaps the "Is it true?" question is relevant for you as you feel a shift in relationship with your place. Are you having a negative reaction to an aspect of your place as a result of personal things going on with you? I distinctly remember needing to get used to single mom life quickly and feeling surrounded in my place by couples and nuclear families. I had changed, my life had changed, and it was time to go.

Second, you have to consider who really changed—was it you? Or was it the place? And are there ways to overcome those changes with different offerings of that place? Perhaps you could reengage in activities that once made you love where you live? Or try new ones that better suit your way of life? I needed to figure out if I could find community in my place considering my newly found single-parent status.

Sometimes your bond weakens for a time. You will have bad days in a place, even in your Place Match. But one bad week in a place doesn't mean it's over, just like one fight doesn't equal divorce. If the match is sustainable—like a marriage—it'll bounce back. But you may have to be reminded why this is where you belong, why you fell in love with the place initially. One way to reignite that love, is to have a staycation, or go back to the dating stage and try to rediscover your place all over again. It's not unlike the "date nights" people go on with their spouses. It's a means of reconnecting, enjoying a place (or a person), and maybe learning something new about them or re-membering something you may have forgotten.

AN EXAMPLE: JANE'S WALK

Jane's Walk is a great way to rediscover your place. Jane's Walk started in 2007 and has become a global program in a very short time. As I wrote in Chapter 6, it started as a way to honor the legacy and principles of urban activ-ist and writer Jane Jacobs, who championed the role of residents in visioning their place and often encouraged residents to experience their cities by foot.

The idea is simple: Residents volunteer to lead a walking tour of the place, and people come out to walk alongside other residents to learn and talk about the place they share. Anyone can be a walk leader, and there is no train-ing required. Across the globe, walk leaders have repre-sented every demographic and status in the community from long-time residents to kids, from city planners to new residents, from residents who wanted to show off a little known gem in the community to residents wanting to highlight a problem to spur mobilization. No need for walkers to sign up. They just show up that day, ready to walk, talk and share. It is truly a plug-and-play idea.

When I brought Jane's Walk to my hometown area of Raleigh in 2014, I knew the program would be a great match here. I was fortunate enough to have lots of interest in Jane's Walk from both walk leaders and walkers. Matt Tomasulo, whose Walk Your City story I mentioned previously, agreed to lead a walk of the state-owned Dorothea Dix campus, which Raleigh was trying to acquire to transform into Raleigh's Central Park. Other leaders included historical architects; Raleigh's influential city planner and past American Planning Association President, Mitchell Silver; and a local blogger with a special interest in the history of the downtown's commerce buildings.

"BUT NOTHING PREPARED ME FOR THE WALKS THEM-SELVES. HUNDREDS SHOWED UP TO WALK. HUNDREDS. IT WAS ASTONISHING FOR THE FIRST YEAR OF A PROGRAM. ON TOMASULO'S WALK, RESIDENTS AUDIBLY GASPED AS WE CAME TO A HILLTOP FOR A BEAUTIFUL VIEW OF THE RALEIGH SKYLINE THROUGH TREES AND FIELD."

Needless to say, there was quite the buzz in Raleigh about the walks. A local realtor offered to supply water and odometers and welcome walkers at start sites. The newspaper did a story about it. And as city organizer, I received emails almost daily asking me questions about the program and what they had to do (or even pay!) to join a walk. Imagine their delight when I said: "No charge, no sign-up, just bring yourself and family and neighbors if you like." Talk about openness! Jane Jacobs would have loved it. I know I did.

But nothing prepared me for the walks themselves. Hundreds showed up to walk. Hundreds. It was astonishing for the first year of a program. On Tomasulo's walk, residents audibly gasped as we came to a hilltop for a beautiful view of the Raleigh skyline through trees and field. "This is why we have to make sure this park happens for Raleigh," Tomasulo said. And instantly I saw 130 people become activated to a cause. People would ask me on that walk, "Did you have to get a permit to come here?" "Is it ok that we are here?". This was a public space, and yet people hadn't even known it was theirs to enjoy. But they did now.

On another walk discussing the architectural history of the Capitol area, I saw a young man translating the talk to his moth-

> **"PEOPLE DESPERATELY WANTED A 'DATE NIGHT' WITH THEIR CITY! THEY WERE CRAVING TO LEARN SOMETHING NEW, HEAR A NEW PERSPECTIVE** OR JUST REDISCOVER THE PLACE THEY CALLED HOME. ...SO CROWDS GREW AS WE WALKED. IT WAS TRANSFORMATIONAL AND SPOKE VOLUMES ABOUT HOW RESIDENTS NEED AN EASY AND REGULAR WAY TO RECONNECT WITH THEIR CITY."

er in Spanish. "She just loves this stuff and never has these kinds of opportunities to hear about Raleigh, so I'm happy to do it," he later explained to me. I can be a softy anyway, but there was no denying the lump in my throat.

And I wasn't the only one. When Mitchell Silver saw the crowd of around 200 who came to see him, thank him and hear about the planning history and future of Raleigh, he had tears in his eyes. At every walk stop, he needed a podium and bullhorn, which I didn't have, because nobody anticipated this. So we just looked at each other, shrugged and looked for an elevated surface he could scream from. I couldn't get one picture with everyone in the shot.

People desperately wanted a "date night" with their city! They were craving to learn something new, hear a new perspective or just rediscover the place they called home. As we walked, people passing us would ask, "What is this? Is it a march?" and a walker would reply, "No, we are just walking and learning cool things about Raleigh!" To which the response was often, "Can I just join in?" and people postponed their current plans in downtown to join us. So crowds grew as we walked. It was transformational and spoke volumes about how residents need an easy and regular way to reconnect with their city.

SO WHAT IF YOU CAN'T REVIVE THE RELATION-SHIP?

Now, a great Jane's Walk or date with place might not always do the trick. In some cases, love of place has been gone for a while and can't be reestablished, but leaving isn't an option either for financial or emotional reasons. At least that's a common response I've heard from some long-time residents who don't feel as connected to their place as they once did. They're so embedded in a community—family and friends are there, they've spent years in a job, they own the house they live in, it's all they know (or really want to know). The reality is that some people won't leave even if they've fallen out of love with the place. Divorce just isn't an option. So they'll continue to feel a low attachment to place, may even complain about it, but will stay put and "stuck in place."

> **"AND, FINALLY, IN CASES LIKE MINE, WANTS AND NEEDS SIMPLY CHANGE.** THE PLACE IS SIMPLY NO LONGER RIGHT FOR US. SO, IF YOU WANT TO FIND YOUR PLACE MATCH, YOU HAVE TO BE WILLING TO SAY GOODBYE."

In other cases, a place may have never lived up to what we wanted from it or hoped for it. This can happen for a lot of reasons. Maybe it was discovered the hard way that vacationing in a place really is different than living there. The place could be a hard nut to crack—meaning it just took too long to feel welcomed, to not feel like an outsider in that place, but to feel at home. During the Soul project, many young people told us that it was important for them to actually be invited to stay in a place by other residents, especially in college towns. They needed to hear that they could make a difference in that place, that they were needed and wanted there.

Welcomeness is created in many ways, as I've said, but most people won't wait forever for the place to fulfill its promise.

And, finally, in cases like mine, wants and needs simply change. The place is simply no longer right for us.

So, if you want to find your Place Match, you have to be willing to say goodbye.

CHAPTER 8

IT'S **OVER**

During my separation from my husband, I remember wondering if I was just taking out my failing marriage on my place. Maybe I was just less happy in general, which wouldn't make it a huge surprise that I was not as happy in Miami.

This is a common thing we do in relationships. We blame ourselves. And sometimes that means we get stuck in relationships or marriages that aren't right for us. That can happen in places too. That's why it's sometimes best to admit it's over and free ourselves to move on.

How I knew my Place Match had really shifted—that it wasn't just my separation sadness—was when I started to adjust to my new normal as a single parent and yet my unhappiness in my place continued. If it was a salvageable Place Match, I should have felt a rebound with the place when I started to feel better about my life circumstances. Instead, I became more convinced that Miami wasn't my place.

> **"THIS IS A COMMON THING WE DO IN RELATIONSHIPS.** WE BLAME OURSELVES. AND SOMETIMES THAT MEANS WE GET STUCK IN RELATIONSHIPS OR MARRIAGES THAT AREN'T RIGHT FOR US. THAT CAN HAPPEN IN PLACES TOO."

Those feelings were especially apparent as I made more trips home to see my parents in Jamestown, North Carolina. They provided support and a safe place when my

"IT MAKES ME THINK OF THE SHOW *EVERYBODY LOVES RAYMOND.* RAYMOND'S PARENTS ALWAYS JOKED ABOUT HOW MUCH THEY WANTED TO GET AWAY FROM EACH OTHER. AND IT WOULD BEG THE QUESTION: IF THEY WERE REALLY THAT MISERABLE, WHY WERE THEY STILL TOGETHER?"

marriage was falling apart. As we traveled around the area to provide Grace fun things to do (and for me to take some deep breaths), I found myself not wanting to leave North Carolina to go back home. As I was feeling that disconnection from Miami, I was reconnecting with my home state.

Because job and marriage were no longer keeping me in Miami, I really had to love it to stay. And it was increasingly clear that I didn't. I became determined that my new life circumstances would not deter me from the plan to move back to North Carolina.

STUCK IN PLACE

I'm fortunate to have had the freedom to leave and go find my new Place Match. The hardest stories for me to hear during my travels are about those who feel stuck in place, for whatever reason. Often these people (usually older residents) prefer what they know over the unknown of a new place, or they just don't have the economic means to leave.

It makes me think of the show *Everybody Loves Raymond.* Raymond's parents always joked about how much they wanted to get away from each other. And it would beg the question: if they were really that miserable, why were they still together? Or, was joking about how much they disliked their life together part of their narrative? Was it how their relationship worked?

Either way, Raymond's parents' discourse is representative of life choices 30 to 40 years ago. According to Marie (Raymond's mother), "Hatred is a part of any marriage. You just put your head down and plow through to the next moment." But in many relationships and marriages today—just like in places today—we'll only take so many moments of unhappiness before we're just done. We generally lack the same commitment of our grandparents' marriages. When the relationship isn't working for us, we become most committed to finding a way out. Personal happiness and fulfillment are much more prioritized, right or wrong.

Seeing people stuck in place is really the hardest for me to witness. That's because the barriers that keep them there are real and not easily solved. And the sadness or even loss they express when they talk about their places is poignant.

DECISION TIME FOR THOSE STUCK IN PLACE

There are usually two outcomes in this scenario. One happens when the feelings of unhappiness with place spread and become so pervasive that they negatively affect the overall community dynamic. The place suffers, as do the people in it.

The other is when residents who aren't in love with their place stay and make the best of it. They live with some level of place incompatibility, knowing it's not their ultimate Place Match. But they find happiness where they can in their place and focus on that.

So what's your choice? Are you going to make the best of your place and maybe never find the fulfillment of a Place Match? Or are you willing to search for your Place Match, perhaps again and again as your needs change, even as you suffer place disappointments along the way? Is it better to have loved and lost than never to have loved at all?

It is a choice you must make. And you will, whether actively or passively. Each path has its own happiness and heartbreak, its own pros and cons. In the end, your choice may be more about who you are than where you live.

But if you do decide to leave, know that it's a process—a necessary step to find your match.

You might still feel ties to the place even as you pack up and move. Just like in marriages, you might have children to consider. You have to recognize what a move means to them, and help them through the transition. There are financial implications of selling your home (while simultaneously trying to find another one), changing jobs, moving, etc. You have to prepare to leave and assist those you love with the upcoming change to a new normal. All that takes time, effort and planning.

Moving on doesn't always mean moving straight into a

new Place Match, either. You might want to find refuge after saying goodbye to a place. Maybe it's in an escape place—a place with friends, family or other social support. Or maybe it's simply a transition place where that new round of soul searching can happen.

GETTING OKAY WITH "IT'S OVER"

"It's over" doesn't have to be sad. Sometimes leaving a place happens because you're retiring to a relaxing

"MOVING ON DOESN'T ALWAYS MEAN MOVING STRAIGHT INTO A NEW PLACE MATCH EITHER. YOU MIGHT WANT TO FIND REFUGE AFTER SAYING GOODBYE TO A PLACE—A PLACE WITH FRIENDS, FAMILY OR OTHER SOCIAL SUPPORT."

and tropical place that you've dreamed about for most of your working life. It could mean a move closer to family in order to age alongside those you love or to care for young grandchildren. A new place could also represent the start of a new marriage. If you dated a person from a distance, saying goodbye to your old place might mean hello to a new life and new city with the person you love.

And yet, sometimes moving on is unnatural or forced. It's not that you've fallen out of love with your place, but your circumstances changed. A job is forcing a move. Or you lost a job and can't afford to stay in your home or your place. Maybe your elderly parents need you to be closer to them. Maybe your house was significantly damaged by a natural disaster, and you just can't afford to rebuild there. Something external can affect your relationship with your place and make it time to move on. Having to leave a place you love, a "forced divorce," is hard. It's not the way you want it to be, and yet, it just is. This is how I felt about my own marriage, and it's a special kind of heartbreak.

"HAVING TO LEAVE A PLACE YOU LOVE, A 'FORCED DIVORCE,' IS HARD. IT'S NOT THE WAY YOU WANT IT TO BE, AND YET, IT JUST IS. THIS IS HOW I FELT ABOUT MY OWN MARRIAGE, AND IT'S A SPECIAL KIND OF HEARTBREAK."

City leaders need to be okay with residents saying goodbye. They have to realize that residents have to do what's best for them. Philadelphia's Mayor Michael Nutter first raised that point to me during a Knight Soul meeting in 2010, shortly after I separated from my husband. He basically said, "If we are trying to be our authentic best as a place and effectively demonstrate who we are as a place and that doesn't fit with someone, then it's best we part. We have to become comfortable with keeping people and losing people." Then he added, "If somebody doesn't want you for you, then so be it." I had to remind myself if we were talking about places or partners.

Nutter recognizes that mobility is okay and even useful sometimes. A large percentage of stuck in place residents can be hard on a city, as I've said. Nutter wants residents who love Philadelphia, those who believe it's the place for them and will use that love as motivation to help continue to optimize the place. And their contributions will help Philadelphia maximize its readiness for new residents looking for a match.

But if you believe that our environments impact our quality of life and fulfillment—as research and, increasingly, many people do—then sometimes saying goodbye is the only way to free yourself to find your next Place Match.

CHAPTER 9

ANOTHER
CHANCE

Moving on from a place doesn't have to be doom and gloom. I hope that was evident in the last chapter. In this one, I want to be clear why moving on can be good, or perhaps a blessing in disguise.

It's a lot like after the end of a relationship or divorce. As the mourning and sadness subside, there's time to do a post mortem on the experience. Reevaluate yourself, your role in the relationship, what you've learned and how you may be different coming out the other side than when you entered the relationship.

As difficult as any loss can be, there is also a sense of freedom that can be useful and healing. Don't hurry through the steps. Just like it's not a good idea to jump into another relationship after a breakup. This is a time for reflection, for considering where the relationship succeeded and where it failed, for determining what is now different about you and what you should do differently in your next search, or what you want differently in your place.

Then, when you're ready, go through the steps I've outlined all over again. Date. Choose. Embrace your Place Match.

FINDING A NEW PLACE MATCH CAN TAKE TIME

Though I knew my Place Match was North Carolina, I didn't know what city I wanted to live in, or what neighborhood. I didn't know where I'd find new friends, or where was best for my daughter to go to school and get connected.

My previous time in North Carolina went like this: I grew up in the small town of Jamestown then moved to Raleigh to go to college and stayed nearby when I went to graduate school at the University of North Carolina at Chapel Hill. I knew a lot about many places in North Carolina, but my knowledge about the specifics of the places was 10 years old. Even though I knew it was the state for me, I had to relearn my Place Match before I made a permanent commitment. This was one of the reasons that I rented a home when I moved back to North Carolina.

Another reason? I needed to figure out what home really meant for me. In Miami, we lived in a townhouse and then in a high-rise condominium. Valet drivers parked our cars and our groceries were delivered to our unit. We had 24-hour security officers who called us for approval when friends came to visit. We had a view of the yacht club from our west balcony and a view of the pools, the Intracoastal Waterway and the ocean from our east balcony. My mom once commented that it was like living in a hotel, which I initially thought was a compliment, but upon reflection, realized was

> **"I KNEW A LOT ABOUT MANY PLACES IN NORTH CAROLINA, BUT MY KNOWLEDGE ABOUT THE SPECIFICS OF THE PLACES WAS 10 YEARS OLD.** EVEN THOUGH I KNEW IT WAS THE STATE FOR ME, I HAD TO RELEARN MY PLACE MATCH BEFORE I MADE A PERMANENT COMMITMENT."

probably her way of saying it didn't feel like a home.

And though we paid dearly for the condo, there never was enough space. I tried to contain the baby paraphernalia after Grace was born, but it was everywhere. My husband and I also tried to share a home office. Even once it was just Grace and I (yes, I spent two difficult years in our family home in Miami after my husband and I split), space was still a precious commodity.

When she was about 3 years old, I remember Grace asking the building's landscapers if she could have a small space in the front of the building to plant a garden. Although it was amusing to see landscapers explain the concepts of "homeowners' associations" and "common space" to a preschooler, it planted the seed of what I would seek in North Carolina.

When I came back to North Carolina, I debated between Charlotte and Raleigh and ultimately decided on Cary, a growing town just outside Raleigh with a strong family-friendly and place-centered reputation. Next, I had to find a neighborhood within Cary (which was a lot bigger than it had been 10 years earlier). I was very conscious of my single-mom status and wanted to find a neighborhood that was welcoming. I wanted access to social offerings that would appeal to my daughter and me. I also became acutely aware that I would be responsible for all chores and maintenance, and eventually the repairs and upkeep. I had to think about what kind of home I would take on.

But louder was the voice inside me that wanted a home in a neighborhood, with more space than I needed, and of course, a yard that was plantable. I still needed to try all that out before I took it on permanently.

So I rented. For three years.

I often preach that we have to get rid of the stigma around renting. In the past, homeowners were the desirables and renters were not. Homeowners were more likely to keep up the aesthetics of their home and join the neighborhood watch, to become loyal visitors to local shops, restaurants, salons, physicians and other businesses, all of which help the local economy. Renters were not as loyal.

The Soul project went a long way in indicating a new reality when it came to renters. It showed that community attachment is not the purview of just homeowners. Sometimes the renters were more attached than homeowners.

Turns out that some people are like me—they are just not ready for a new commitment yet. They're unsure and still thinking it through. If you aren't sure where you fit in your new place—if you're still dating it to be sure it's right, then don't make the long-term commitment of purchasing a home quite yet.

ADJUSTING TO THE NEW NORMAL

I was fortunate to find a home to rent a mile from an elementary school in one of the best neighborhoods in Cary. It boasted four bedrooms, three-and-a-half baths, a playroom, an office and a front and back yard with a garden and a swingset. But I soon realized that I was basically the only single person in the neighborhood, certainly on my street.

And that brought the questions from neighbors about where I was moving from and why. This was a tough one for me—I believe the question of why you moved from one place to another is as personal as asking why someone got divorced or split up. The answer you provide will often invite judgment, and that is why so many of us give very sanitized responses to the question. Not so lucky for me, those answers were intertwined. Though I was only just starting to admit I was separated, I used this time to practice saying it. It was also a test to see how welcoming my nuclear-family neighbors would be. I'm grateful to say that they were delightfully inclusive of us.

> **"I BELIEVE THE QUESTION OF WHY YOU MOVED FROM ONE PLACE TO ANOTHER IS AS PERSONAL AS ASKING** WHY SOMEONE GOT DIVORCED OR SPLIT UP. THE ANSWER YOU PROVIDE WILL OFTEN INVITE JUDGMENT, AND THAT IS WHY SO MANY OF US GIVE VERY SANITIZED RESPONSES TO THE QUESTION."

As I closed out my three years in my rental home, I learned a lot about the area and the place. We were close to the neighborhood pool, a short bike ride to the nearby lake and walking distance to the elementary school. I was 20 minutes (or less) from the international airport, 90 minutes from my parents, 15 minutes from Grace's dad and an easy drive to farmers markets, decent grocery stores and parks. I also hung my own Christmas lights from the roof, hauled trash, replaced light bulbs, learned how to light the pilot light in the gas fireplace, survived summer storms, ice storms and power outages and planned and hosted Grace's birthday parties in that home.

Grace and I grew our own tomatoes and witnessed our first bird nest in the yard. I regrew confidence in myself and in my place.

> **"WHEN WE MOVE ON, WE HAVE TO ADMIT THAT THERE WASN'T NECESSARILY ANYTHING 'WRONG' WITH THE PLACE WE LIVED BEFORE.** ...BUT NOW THAT'S OVER. THERE'S A NEW NORMAL, NEW YOU, NEW REALITY."

When we move on, we have to admit that there wasn't necessarily anything "wrong" with the place we lived before. It still might be perfect for our friends or family who stayed behind (I still have friends in Miami who absolutely love it).

After all, it was the place for us for a time too—we chose it, designated it our Place Match (or made the best of it) and stayed. But now that's over. There's a new normal, new you, new reality.

And that's okay.

You can have another chance to find your Place Match.

CHAPTER 10

CREATING
A GOOD
PARTNERSHIP

Throughout this book, I hope you've found some relatable anecdotes and tactical tips for finding, knowing and analyzing your Place Match. But I'd be remiss if I didn't leave you with some real ways of optimizing your match once you're in it. This chapter is for that.

The relationship you have with your Place Match should be like that of any solid marriage. For any marriage to work, both people have to be good partners. They should recognize and play to each other's strengths, know and assist in each other's challenges and stay engaged with each other and in the marriage along the way.

In a place, that means that both the residents and the place commit to each other in word and deed. The residents get involved in their place, and their commitment is especially evident when times aren't as good. Another party plays a supporting role too: the city leaders. They are kind of like a mother-in-law in any marriage—hopefully, they support the partnership between people and their place rather than being obstructive and controlling.

Here's how to be a good partner to your place and recognize the kind of leadership you have contributing to your relationship.

STAY CONNECTED

In today's world, we keep marriages fresh by having date nights with our spouse. We leave behind kids and work and chores and responsibilities and commit a night every so often to keep our marriages from getting stale or routine.

A staycation is the another kind of "date night" for places. During a staycation, you visit your town's best attractions, stay in a local hotel and dine at restaurants nearby. If you've wanted to check out a new museum exhibit or a minor league baseball game or a local water park or a top chef's new cuisine, a staycation is a great time for those experiences.

You go into a weekend or week or even a single night with the same mindset as you would a vacation—that it's time to have fun and experience something new in a relaxed and undistracted way. The only difference is you stay right at home to do it.

"BUT STAYING CONNECTED TO YOUR PLACE ISN'T ALWAYS ABOUT CELEBRATING THE GOOD. IT'S ALSO ABOUT FACING THE BAD, AND CHOOSING TO JUMP IN AND IMPROVE IT. IN RELATIONSHIPS, IF ONE DAY IS ROUGH, GOOD PARTNERS WORK TO MAKE THE NEXT DAY BETTER."

Staycations are a critical way to see the best in your place, and stay in love with it over time. One of the things we saw during the Knight Soul project is that many residents didn't have the disposable income to vacation, likely due to the economic crisis happening during that time. They ended up spending more time in their cities. And those cities that offered an enjoyable staycation option, even if it was a forced staycation, reaped the rewards of increased attachment. Those who didn't took a hit in resident attachment.

Cities rarely could do anything more or different to further attach their residents during that time—they couldn't afford to—and were happy if they could just maintain their status quo. But the recession forced residents to stay home and rediscover their place and some were impressed with what they found. It was a win-win for place and residents during what was otherwise a very difficult time.

But staying connected to your place isn't always about celebrating the good. It's also about facing the bad, and choosing to jump in and improve it. In relationships, if one day is rough, good partners work to make the next day better. They recognize positive qualities even while they accept shortcomings and try to stay supportive regardless of which is on display.

In your place, you might not like every new development idea. You might worry about school quality. You might not like some of the headlines you read about local crime. You might second-guess your leadership's authenticity or intentions. Let your love of place guide you in sticking it out. Even better, allow it to inspire you to get involved and be part of the solution.

Part of being a good partner is also accepting that some things about our place we can't change, and we can't expect to change just because we don't like it. Nobody is perfect. And no place is perfect. The best we can hope for is that our Place Match is the perfect place for us, and that means warts and all.

Even when we show off our best selves—our city hosts a great event, its sports team has a winning season or the weather is just perfect for days at a time—there will always be problems. Your love of place should be strong enough that you want to take care of the place during the rough times and celebrate during the great ones.

Our goal with places should not be perfection, but resiliency. Resiliency is the ability to identify and solve problems and challenges successfully. It is that "secret sauce" you see at work in places that seem to almost magically get things done, while other places struggle. And I believe that resilience comes when residents are attached to the place enough that they feel tied to its success. The lines between "my life" and "place life" are so blurred that the challenges or problems of place inspire residents to seek common ground and find solutions.

Again, the same is true for marriage. Your goal shouldn't be to have the perfect marriage, but to have a resilient one—one that can withstand conflict, job changes, children, financial stress and other hardships that will inevitably happen. In this kind of marriage, you stay focused on the common ground and the love that brought you together in the first place to build strategies to overcome what life throws your way.

BE INVOLVED

Just like in a marriage, your relationship with place is not only about what the place does for you, it is about what you do for the place. By your mere presence, you contribute to the culture and attitude of the place. And by your actions, you contribute to problem-solving (or creation), civility (or lack thereof) and engagement (or apathy). These are choices you make in big and little ways that accumulate over time as your contribution to the place.

If you care about the aesthetics in your community, you can do the traditional engagement activities of joining a neighborhood council or organizing a community clean-up. Or you can teach your children about littering and be a part of the family recycling efforts. Visit your local parks to show community leadership that these places matter to you. Designate your backyard as a NestWatch site. Make daily choices to honor green space in your community.

> **"JUST LIKE IN A MARRIAGE, YOUR RELATIONSHIP WITH PLACE IS NOT ONLY ABOUT WHAT THE PLACE DOES FOR YOU,** IT IS ABOUT WHAT YOU DO FOR THE PLACE. BY YOUR MERE PRESENCE, YOU CONTRIBUTE TO THE CULTURE AND ATTITUDE OF THE PLACE."

Welcomeness and openness in a place greatly depends on you too. You can go the traditional route and join the Welcome Wagon (yes, this and versions of this still exist). Or put your own spin on it. Help someone reach something on a high shelf at the grocery store. Tip a newcomer or visitor to a hidden gem spot in your community. Discuss the joys and tribulations of parenting at the sandbox with a parent you don't know. Lay off your horn on the roads.

Increasingly, there are groups designed to assist you in this area—We Should Know Each Other, EatWith and Feastly provide a vehicle for you to become more welcoming and to have that welcomeness extended to you as well by having residents host events in their home for others. Demonstrate this to your children too, and encourage them to seek friends widely. Remember you are sharing your Place Match with others who are somewhere on their own Place Match journey as well. That's great common ground to start.

> **"YOUR PARTNERSHIP WITH YOUR PLACE MATCH IS A THREE-LEGGED STOOL COMPRISED OF:** (1) WHAT THE PLACE PROVIDES YOU, (2) WHAT YOU PROVIDE THE PLACE, AND (3) WHAT THE LEADERSHIP PROVIDES IN FACILITATING YOUR PARTNERSHIP".

Lastly, be social. Participate in local events, and invite people to join you. You can volunteer to help design these events, or just be a happy participant. Your Place Match connection thrives when you're active in your place, so getting out there in it is key.

Your involvement doesn't have to take a lot of time or money. It's just about making pro-place contributions in big and small ways every day. What is it that you're willing to do to make your place a better place? Think about it, and then start doing it.

KNOW YOUR MOTHER-IN-LAW

My best advice for mayors and other place leaders, the facilitators of the Place Match relationship, is to help make it a healthy one. In that sense, place leaders are like the mother-in-law. Common complaints against mothers-in-law are that they are just too much—obtrusive, meddling, overbearing. Or, they are not enough—not supportive, not helpful, not accountable, not useful. The best mothers-in-law are just enough—they foster a good relationship between their adult child and his or her spouse by providing support and a helping hand when needed without being omnipresent and a know-it-all.

As a resident, you should be aware of what kind of leadership you have. Pay attention to how your leaders operate in the place. Do they listen to the residents and then create policy or create programs to meet needs or solve problems? Or do they do what they think is best for a place without seeking that kind of advice and feedback? Are they good about "getting to yes" when residents want something to happen? Do they communicate effectively the direction of the place and inspire optimism? Do they make it easy for residents to interact with them and the place, or do they prefer the red tape and ivory towers? Are they really supportive of your relationship with your place, or do you really wish they'd just get out of the way?

A mother-in-law as facilitator is a powerful role in any marriage partnership, or any Place Match. My former mother-in-law wrote on our signable engagement picture frame: "Love. Change. Growth." Those are the elements at work all the time in your relationship with your partner and with your place. It's how you handle them that will determine your outcome. A leader who recognizes those elements and successfully manages them can be your ally in your Place Match along the way.

Your partnership with your Place Match is a three-legged stool comprised of: (1) what the place provides you, (2) what you provide the place, and (3) what the leadership provides in facilitating your partnership. Being mindful of all legs at work in your Place Match will help facilitate a solid partnership, enable you to monitor its health over time and foster resilience.

CHAPTER 11

CONCLUSION

Where you choose to live is among the most important decisions in your life, and this book gives you the freedom to think of it that way. I hope that it also provides some tactical tips for finding your Place Match.

Like any other field, mine has its fair share of jargon. Words and phrases like "placemaking" and "resident attachment" are just not part of everyday language yet. Since I began speaking about the Knight Soul project, I have tested out a variety of ways to talk about issues of place, in hopes of helping people understand, relate and apply our research and learnings.

I have asked audiences to think about how they show off their place when people visit them, a way to get them to think about what attaches them to the place. I've talked about love of place instead of "attachment."

But it wasn't until an off-the cuff-remark I made during that keynote in Canada a few years back that I found a perspective that made all of the place concepts relatable. That finding, choosing and living in a place is a lot like finding, choosing and then making a life with a partner and that attachment to a place is like the love and commitment of marriage. It's a way to reorganize the way we think and talk about place.

In many ways, it's a refresh of the Soul project, now well over five years old. Don't get me wrong—the project is still relevant today. People are still fascinated by the detailed findings of those three years of work. It still helps to guide my work with cities. It's still what folks want to hear about.

But I believe Place Match is a much more relatable way to

understand place dynamics, especially for residents. When I talk about dating your place, committing to it or leaving it in a relationship context, the concepts just make sense to people. It validates the feelings they have about their place and gives a framework for making decisions about where to live.

Place Match has certainly made sense to me as my life has paralleled much of what I talk about in this book.

Just a few months since I started writing this book, I'm in my Place Match. In April 2015, I moved into the house I'd spent two years searching for. It's 1.8 miles from the rental home and neighborhood Grace and I came to love since moving from Miami. It's walkable from Grace's elementary school, and close to other destinations we love and frequent in Cary.

"I HAVE FOUND MY PLACE MATCH AND LEARNED A LOT ABOUT MYSELF ALONG THE WAY. THE SAME WILL BE TRUE FOR YOU. I ENCOURAGE YOUR JOURNEY AND HOPE THIS BOOK HAS GIVEN YOU A USEFUL ROADMAP AS A GUIDE. FOR FINDING YOUR PLACE MATCH IS A VITAL PART OF LIVING YOUR BEST LIFE."

Just as importantly, it symbolizes all the things I value about place. I've mentioned before its large wooded lot, one of the last of its kind in Cary. It also has a smell of pine and a veranda that overlooks the natural beauty that is so quintessentially North Carolina to me. Deer and rabbits regularly pass through our yard. And because of the wooded natural habitat, scientists from the local museum use our yard as a regular site to tag and track various bird species and their nests. One of our favorite features is a deck that's built around a 100-year-old pine tree, honoring what came before our community was covered in homes and businesses.

I'd driven by this house many times, always noticing its charm and setting but figuring no one would ever leave a house or property like that.

When it became available, I'd nearly given up on my search for the perfect home and I figured I'd end up with a quarter-acre lot in a newer subdivision in another neighborhood. After much exploring and trying to follow the guidelines I've set out in this book, I'm delighted to say I found my Place Match.

There was this house, and then every other house. I knew we wouldn't find another like it.

So, I found my Place Match and learned a lot about myself along the way. The same will be true for you. I encourage your journey and hope this book has given you a useful roadmap as a guide. For finding your Place Match is a vital part of living your best life.

Where you live affects all aspects of your life, just like any other partner choice. So choose wisely with your heart and your head and strive to make it work once you've committed to it.

If you still don't succeed in either partnership or if it seems lost over time, don't lose hope. Embrace each stage of this journey and know you are right where you are supposed to be in finding where you belong.

ACKNOWLEDGMENTS

I am very appreciative to all who encouraged me to write this book and helped me to make it a reality.

Acknowledgements to the John S. and James L. Knight Foundation which not only was a great supporter of my early career and my attainment of my doctorate, but also provided me (and the world!) with such a great opportunity and gift with the Knight Soul of the Community project.

A heartfelt thanks to all of my clients and partner cities around the world. I am always honored to be welcomed and trusted with your personal journeys with place. I have learned so much from you.

Thanks to my colleagues who have lifted me up and supported my work in service of place ever since I first came on the scene. A special thanks to my placemaking BFF, Mitchell Silver, who wrote a spot-on foreword for this book. Thanks also to Joe Borgstrom, Chuck Wolfe, Ethan Kent, Fred Kent, Craig Pollett, Tigran Haas, Paula Ellis, Meredith Hector, Bud Meyer, Mike Poller, Matt Tomasulo, Michael

Barranda, Quinn Pettifer, Chad Simmons, Jeff Pomeranz, Neil Dawe and Axiom News. Thanks also to my Facebook colleagues and Twitter followers who read my blogs and musings and share with me in return.

Thanks to my book team for helping me see this project through. Laura Baverman, who helped turn a speaker into an author, and the whole team at Story Farm, who guided and encouraged this book to completion and praised it once it was done. Thanks also to the local community theater talent who made my book promotional trailers come to life on screen.

I am blessed to have a wonderful inner circle. Dee Dee Dunlap, who helped me through some of the roughest times in my life, supports me unconditionally, but still tells me The Truth when I need to hear it. That is the best kind of friend to have. With related thanks to Jeff Dunlap who always has my back in all things great and small. Thanks to all of my other friends near and far, from childhood to today, who each have contributed as only they could to making my life an easier, funnier, happier, kinder and overall more fulfilling experience. You have all let it be known, even if from a distance, that Grace and I are loved.

A special gratitude to my parents, Esther and Dan Loflin, who have encouraged and supported me through my schooling, my career and my (sometimes tumultuous) life. And a very special thanks to my mom, who has done everything possible to help me seek my greatest potential. It is a profound gift and I am fortunate.

Thanks to Richard for being okay with me talking about the most difficult part of our lives together in this book. But also for my greatest gift: our daughter, Grace.

Grace is defined as "the benevolent favor of God." And that's what you have been to me. You are undoubtedly the reason I became the best me I could be. So lastly, thank you, Grace, for naming me the "City Doctor," for giving me countless stories and insights that I get to share with the world, for our forever bond...and for calling me a superhero—the feeling is mutual. It is my privilege to be your mother. I can't wait to witness all you will do with your life.